Puzzle Pieces

Nate Taylor

BookLeaf Publishing

Presentation by *BookLeaf Publishing*

Web: www.bookleafpub.com

E-mail: info@bookleafpub.com

ISBN: 9789357210812

First edition 2022

DEDICATION

For Michele, for understanding me more than I understand myself and loving be regardless

For Ellie, that you may grow and cherish those formative years in a way that your father never did

PREFACE

Within this book are a series of poems from throughout my formative years that helped me get through some dark and difficult times. By God's grace, I have overcome many trials and am happy to say that I no longer dwell within the despair that several of these works thrive in; however, to deny that pieces of me remain within them in some fashion would be denying my very being. Though they are not perfect and though many are not even good, I believe that publishing these poems is a necessary step in overcoming the demons of my past and moving on with my life. For those that knew me then and were affected by my own misery, I truly am sorry.

Charlotte

What happens to a dream pursued?

Does it sprout up
like a flower from the ground?
Or flourish like a spring -
And then abound?
Does it smell like autumn rain?
Or flow and ripple outward -
like a wide, rolling plain.

Maybe it's secure
like a humble abode.

Or does it implode?

Who I Am

Who is he?
He's the kind of guy who calls everybody a friend.
Ecstatic expressions and goofy grins are his clothing of choice;
Wisecracks and wit are his currency, and he always pays in full.
Both empathetic and imaginative, his emotions run deep and his dreams soar wide.
A bold introvert or a shy extrovert, no one can really tell.
There is charisma and confidence that shines brighter than a lighthouse,
Shining through the darkness on the stormy seas...
But lighthouses only rest on rocky shores,
warning those in passing of the danger beneath its beams.

Who is he really?
He's the kind of guy who never knows who to call a friend.
Depreciating doubt and solemn smiles are his clothing of circumstance;

Loathing and lament are his penance, and he always pays in full.
Both self-critical and realistic, his resentment runs deep and his pessimism soars wide.
A broken extrovert or a lousy introvert, no one can really tell.
There is agony and anxiety that protrudes sharper than a rocky shore,
Denying ships a safe haven from the stormy seas...
But rocky shores always have a lighthouse, giving hope to those in passing with the brightness of its beams.

So which is it?
Who is he?
He is both and neither; he is one and the other.
He walks the line between heaven and hell and struggles to find balance.
As symmetrical as this story, he is split down the middle of two extremes,
Continually free falling through the limbo in between.
But the question stands:
Who is he?

He is me.

A Fractured Heart

Beauty true and beauty free
Captivating from the start
Beauty clung my soul to thee
Refuge for this fractured heart

As our love grew tenderly
In a blooming work of art
So my soul was bound to thee
Comforting this fractured heart

But emotions as they be
Wildly did play a part
Caused this wandering mind to flee
And retreat my fractured heart

Ever I so foolishly
Chose to viciously depart
Yet you clung so desperately
To this failing fractured heart

Passion rampant as the sea
Pressure longing to restart
Foolish actions made by me
Left you with a fractured heart

So I suffer silently
Masking pain in rhythmic art
Longing for my soul to see
Beauty in this fractured heart

Bittersweet be memory
Though in life we grow apart
In my dreams eternally
You're within this fractured heart

Ghosts of Tiananmen

I look around me - chaos, turmoil...destruction.
My vision is blurred; my hearing is muffled.
I am disoriented.
But I can see the terror perfectly clear;
The horrific screams ring in my aching ears.
I look at the people around me - confusion, horror...regret.
To my left, a woman holds the bleeding body of a man.
She releases a shrill cry for help as tears rush from her eyes...but no one helps her.
To my right, a young boy paces nervously, stricken pale from the sight.
He yells for his mother...but she will never return to him.
I look at the place around me - stark, frightening...lifeless.
Soulless bodies lie still, soaking in the warm, crimson rain.
Breathing corpses flee the scene, blindly running from the metal stampede.
A wall of flames engulfs the square; a choice is given to we who stand:
A scorching death or merciless slaughter.
There is no escaping the fate we face.

I look at the people before me - harsh,
relentless...monstrous.
A line of smoking barrels march forward,
crushing bikes as well as bones.
With them fly blazing bullets, firing with every
intention to kill.
Every round devours flesh; every shot consumes
a life.
But there is no mercy here...
Peace is dead; freedom, a myth.
All hope we once had for life has shattered
beneath their boots.
I look at the panic around me - chaos,
turmoil...destruction.
I fall to my knees.
A sudden rush of pain fills my body.
I look around...there is no escape.
No refuge.
No shelter.
No haven to keep us safe.
I look down to see my hand drenched in my own
blood...
I slowly rest upon the ground.
I breathe heavily.
My prison has become my only sanctuary.
I feel the currents.
I see the terror.
I hear the screams.

I close my eyes, silently praying for this all to end.
My vision fades completely; my hearing is entirely gone.
I am disoriented.
I fall into the dark silence,
And I finally rest...

A Song of Stars

Celestial sparkles in the sky
Carefully they Twinkle up above
Gallivanting in the blackness of night
Generously they Twinkle against the dark
All their Little lights aglow
All of them a Star, all a beacon
Grasping after tomorrow

Forever present, dim by day
Feverish How they flicker on
Each night, I Wonder their aim
Each night, I wonder What is their purpose
Do You beckon our attention heavenward?
Do you eternalize the gods of old?
Careful considerations Are all around

Gallantly glaring upward
Gazing Up Above The globe
Far above this World we love
Far above our humble home
Ever shining, So you are
Ever upward, High up in the sky
Do you look down as we look up?

Glory of ye heavenly host
Give us answers that we seek
For we long to know your purpose
For we long to know your secrets
Each night, I wonder your goal
Each night, you still appear Like A
Diamond In The Sky

Celestial sparkles way up high
Confidently they Twinkle together
Gracious brightness in the blackness
Gracefully they Twinkle on
All shining, Little lights
All a Star burning bright
Glowing along the dark skies

Forever How you watch over head
Forever I Wonder your purpose
Each night, What beauty You display
Each night, I wish that you would stay
Do you look down upon us?
Do you wonder what we Are as well?
Celestial lights, never fade away...

The Reaper's Umbrage

Down in sleeping Sombertown
The Reaper came today.
He came for one and one alone
To take his life away.

With His umbrage, close behind
There came Nihility;
And too, behind his other side,
There followed Apathy.

Their shadows like a virus spread
Unbridled o'er the land;
Undulating darkness crept
Within Death's cold, gnarled hand.

He gleaned the cruel and vile souls
Of those deserving spite,
Who lived urbane and pious lives
With hearts that hated light.

Unto the tailor's small abode
The Reaper made His way.
Above his bed, the Spirits watched
The ruddy, young man lay.

Astute and resolute was he -
A man of status great.
Unbeknownst to looming doom,
He dreamed not of his fate.

A treacherous shiver crawled down his spine;
He woke with sudden fear.
He gazed, amazed and horror struck -
He knew his end was near.

With unremitting stammering,
The tailor plead his case,
"B-but, I cannot d-die yet, Sir!
I c-cannot leave this place?"

Attrition flushed into his heart;
His will began to give.
The Reaper snapped with harsh retort,
"Why should I let thee live?!"

"W-well, see," said he, with timid voice,
"I've lived a Christian life!
I'm honest, k-kind, I give a lot-"
"Yet sleep with thy neighbor's wife?!"

The Reaper hissed with blazing rage,
"Your hypocrisy is great!
Thy perjury shall cost you dear -
Your sins have sealed your fate!"

"To friends and those who serviced you,
You tried to hide your wrongs,
But I see your shriveled, wicked heart
And know where it belongs!"

Without another word or thought,
His Scythe swung suddenly
Into the heart of tailor damned:
"Now you belong to ME!"

With a mighty roar and vicious laugh,
The Reaper clutched him tight;
With Death's ice grip, he squeezed his neck
And vanished in the night.

Our eerie hero carries on
To take villains away;
He reaps their weak and sinful souls
And keeps them to decay.

The gist of this atypic tale
Is treasure life most dear.
Don't try and cheat your way from death
Or more you'll have to fear.

Live true to what you say and do -
Hypocrites pay the cost;
They hide themselves from loved ones dear

And then their souls are lost.

Death comes for evil, vile hearts
To take their lives away;
And so it went in Sombertown,
When the Reaper came today...

Germanotta

Once again, my heart is aching
To the point of almost breaking

And I can't stop this commotion
That has been set into motion

Love is something very strong
But cannot be handled wrong

Hearts are fragile to the core
Yet they long for so much more

Making that fatal mistake
Is what causes them to break

But true love cannot be swayed
It must play the choice its made

Once the frail heart has connected
At its core, it's unprotected

Now there's nothing there to save
Love from furnishing a grave

In its own hormonal ruse

Death approached on the Muse

Love cannot be taught or tamed
Only severed, bent, or maimed

Learning each and every time
That blind love is but a crime

Of denying one's desire
To be taken by the fire

That is loneliness most grand
Distant from love's soap box stand

Where it tries to speak the truth
That one does not hear in youth

There are some things never learned
And teachings too soon adjourned

We will never, ever find
That true love is only kind

There are ways we should not go
And some things we'll never know

But despite our failing chance
I still long for this romance

The Man with the Metal Bat

I've been here before.
It's always the same scenario.
After a good dream, after retrieving what was once lost or achieving some valuable possession,
I walk home through the backstreet of a quiet neighborhood.
As I stroll down the dirt and gravel path,
My joyous bliss turns to familiar despair as I hear him once again.
I turn to face him, the man that continues to haunt me in my thoughts and dreams.
He is expressionless,
His eyes tinted behind the reflective lenses of his glass,
His long silver and black hair slicked back in perfect form.
The gruff and booming baritone of this frighteningly quiet man utters only one word, a word that sends chills down my spine:
"Bat."
As if on cue, his little girl appears from the shadows nearby.
Her fact is indistinct, hidden behind the locks of her pitch black hair.

She is wearing a pastel sun dress;
She is wielding a worn metal bat.
The faded color and crusted paint show its age;
The crimson streaks and spattered stains show its purpose.
Painful remembrance floods my mind, panicking about what I know will soon occur...

I've been here before.
It's always the same scenario.
Who is this man?
A figment of my corrupt imagination?
A manifestation of my inner demons?
Some long forgotten acquaintance wronged during my days of living in sin?
Or perhaps...
Is it the little girl who is the true enemy?
Is this man simply some golem of her hatred to be used for her sadistic pleasure?
A projection of her inner chaos made flesh?
Who...what...are these people?
Mere seconds of these colliding trains of thought feel like an eternity as I turn away from my pursuer to try and run.
Clinging desperately to my things, I begin to take off in a terrified sprint...
But it happens yet again.

I've been here before.

It's always the same scenario.
My body feels sluggish,
My weight is gradually pressing,
My legs are immediately tired.
As though swimming in slow motion through a mire most foul,
My body struggles and strains to make any movement forward.
In these brief moments that echo as if eternal, I realize...
I have only made one step.
I turn about to see him, to gauge his progress.
I can hear his footsteps so close behind;
I can see the whites of his eyes;
I can see his little girl standing behind him with a grin.
The adrenaline pumps violently into my veins as I futilely throw myself into frantic chaos -
The more I struggle, the less I can move,
Like psychological quicksand forcing me deeper into its abyss with each frightened thought.
I can't escape.
I fall into the gravel, sinking into my own skin like a boulder in the mud.
Flailing about, calling for help, seeking some escape from this all too real nightmare,
I turn to face the sky above...
Only to see the bright glare bouncing off of his glasses as he stands over me,

Bat in hand.
I take a deep breath and stop struggling,
Painfully aware of the horror that is about to come.

All is silent.
All is still.

I've been here before.
It's always the same scenario.
Ringing.
Ringing.
Ringing.
The clanging of church bells in the distance gracefully masks the rhythm of the metal bat breaking my body with each and every swing.
My soul sulks into the gelatinous shell of my pummeled carcass,
Sinking deeper into the ground with every pounding vibration of steel
To skin,
To muscle,
And finally to bone.
Like a hellish metronome driving one to insanity,
The sadistic symphony is kept in perfect time to the beat of this beating.

Flower Sonnet

Upon a warm and gleaming Summer's morn
Amid the forest green and sapphire sky
Within the shadow of the Queen was born
A crimson Rose whose beauty caught my eye
No gaze had met this heavenly delight
No touch this virgin blossom had defiled
But even God could not avert my sight
And plucking thus, the flower's haven riled
Although my longing heart's intentions pure
The hands of Time upon the Rose unwind
Stripped from its roots, the bloom cannot endure
For beauty lost is never paid in kind
    O Flower, thou might shine eternally
    But only if thy bloom remaineth free

A Beautiful Disaster

The human heart is an interesting thing.
It keeps the body systems moving with every pump and pulse,
And even when it's broken,
Even when it aches from the pain of emotional strain,
It just keeps pumping,
Vigorously, full of life.
The shattered frame is scattered;
The splintered pieces fall apart;
The gaping hole from where the arrow pierce
Now bleeds from ripping it out.
It struggles to beat.
It hates to carry on with the pain,
But instinctively, it keeps pumping,
Never resting, never ceasing.
The scattered fragments try to repair themselves.
They pull together and try to heal.
From the outside, they look okay,
But inside...it remains abstract.
The scattered shards that once formed a vibrant heart
Now piece together a cryptic work of art.
Clearly broken and far beyond resurrection,

And yet...within the fragments lies an odd perfection.
They make beauty of discord -
A kaleidoscope makes a marvelous collage of shape and color,
So the shattered human heart remains beautiful in its way.
Despite its flaws,
Despite its defects,
Despite all of the burdens forced upon it...
The fragile heart stays strong.
Messy, broken, suffering, and imperfect,
Yet it maintains its beauty -
A beautiful disaster.

To A Mockingbird

Though crimson Card'nal, cobalt Jay
Be pleasing to the sight
Unparalleled in majesty
The Eagle in its flight

The Peacock and the Paradise
Both beautiful appear
But none my heart rejoice as when
The Mockingbird I hear

His feathered jacket does not shine
His peppered coat doth fade
Instead this songbird's gift from God
Lies in his serenade

This winged polyglot sings out
In tongues not of his own
Both canine, feline, man's machines,
He mimics in his tone

The Finch reminds us, 'tis a sin
To halt his soothing song
His lullaby that hushes babes
Has done mankind no wrong

This merry minstrel of the skies
To his Creator sings
A joyful noise he proudly makes
Unto the King of Kings

The beauty of this Stately bird
Both pleased my eyes and ears
So in a cage I took him home
To sing away my tears

Returning thus, his song began
To quietly dismiss
But soon my heart did realize
That something was amiss

Whatever could have caused this bird
His melody to halt?
But then the answer dawned on me -
It was MY foolish fault!

Oh God! My God! What have I done?
My poor and wretched slave!
I took his home - his joy - and now
He's silent as the grave!

With haste, I freed him from his cell
He fluttered gleefully
And perching on a branch nearby,
I swore he looked at me

He ruffled up his feathered wings
As if prepared to soar
With head held high and beak raised up
He sang his song once more

Again my heart was born anew
To hear his pleasant chord
Behold, the galant Mockingbird!
His tune, at last, restored!

I gave a sigh and bed farewell
For now would be the end
The time had come to say goodbye
To my avian friend

How marvelous his song abounds
Whenever he is free
This lesson taught by Nature's course
Has not been lost on me

To live with glee - O to be free!
This beauty found in life
If joy be caged, shall bring about
Both misery and strife

The purest beauty free remains
And joyously abound
And one may find it if they search

In Nature all around

The Mockingbird still sings his song
He sounds his soft refrain
And when in Nature's caring gaze
I hear his song again

No Comfort

No doctor can amend your broken heart
No counselor can consolation bring
No artist can attend what's torn apart
No poet can remind it how to sing

No father understands the way it breaks
No mother comprehends what has begun
No friend can ever know what all it takes
No bother can reverse the damage done

No person can explain what has been said
No place can push these memories away
No thing can take away the sense of dread
No force can change the words exchanged that day

No number of apologies will do
No action can your bitterness abate
No wish can make all of the lies come true
No feeling can release you from your fate

No hand was there to wipe away your tears
No eyes were there to gaze upon your face
No voice was there to hush away your fears
No arms were there to give a warm embrace

No comfort comes to keep away the pain
No peace of mind is there to see you through
No melody can wash away the stain
No one can ever tell you what to do

When Does A Man Die?

In memory of James Coad, Jr.

When is the moment that a man truly dies?
When he takes his last breath? When the light leaves his eyes?
When the doctor bows his head the family cries?
When reality sets in on those dark, brooding skies?

Perhaps when he's crippled, exhausted, and worn -
That's when most relatives begin to mourn.
Or maybe it happens on the day he is born,
Born into sin and a world bruised and torn.

Is it when he's forgotten and our memories fade?
When his possessions are gone and his debts all repaid?
When the casket is lowered and the earth is relaid?
When a new life is born, do we call it a trade?

Is there something more after life's taken track?
Or is this truly the end with no turning back?

Some dates on a tombstone, our name on a
plaque;
The finale, the climax, the lights fade to black...

But there is a hope for which Christians sing;
To die is to gain and our salvation bring.
"Where is your victory? Death, where is your
string?"
We trust in the promises of our risen King.

He kept the faith and met Christ face to face.
With righteousness crowned in the light of God's
grace,
The heavenly host is now his embrace.
He has fought the good fight, he has finished the
race...

Play Write

"To act, or not to act?"
That is the question -
I can't make up my mind
Or choose the right direction.
My thoughts are all but clear,
So fogged with doubt;
They all seem to say,
"There's no way out..."

"To act, or not to act?"
That is the choice -
Should I pursue the part
Or muffle my voice?
To not, 'twould feel wrong,
But seems the right;
To do feels correct,
Perchance, I might.

"To act, or not to act?"
That's the inquisition -
I must conclude this rhyme
By making my decision.
If I were to act,
It matters not;
She's seemed to move on

And me forgot...

"To act, or not to act?"
That is the question -
Time is up, so thus,
I'm making my selection.
To some it may bring sorrow,
Some may rejoice,
But whatever the reaction,
I've made my choice...

Psychomachia

I'm the guy that everybody wants but nobody needs
Fun to hang out with but not to keep around
Lift everybody up but keep getting let down
I've got a bunch of friends yet none to call my own
I have hope for the future and regrets in the past
I keep trying to improve, but I just can't last
They want to hear my voice but don't want to hear me speak
I'm included in the plans due to pity and guilt
I'm always there for them when they're not there for me
I make plans to visit, but it's not me they want to see
I hate to see them lose; they don't care to see me win
They love me for my good, but they hate me for my sin
They give me hope that I have friends who care about my fate
When all they have are lying hearts of deception and hate
They laugh and they love
And they truly live when my absence is at hand

Who am I to steal away that happiness from them?

Love Lies

Her touch is toxic; her voice, venomous.
One wrong doing is a small matter,
But a plotted spite?
A planned betrayal?
A deceitful facade of interest backed by cruel intent?
What was meant to be a special moment -
One of the few things I looked forward to in life -
Has been stolen from me.
A pleasant dream, raped and murdered.

At first, it looked good; things were going right for once.
Then it unraveled...
Underneath her beautiful exterior it was ugly:
A black heat filled with spite and vengeance.
A white lie that became a blinding monstrosity.
A plot to smash my wandering heart.
Well, it worked.
It was destroyed.

Where my heart once stood remains a pile of rubble.

"One more kiss could be the best thing;
And one more lie could be the worst..."
They were one in the same:
A kiss poisoned with cruel lies.
It meant nothing to her.
Nothing at all.

And though I forgive her,
Wounds can only heal so fast.
The road to recovery is often slow,
And only time can heal wounds so deep.
How many times can this heart put itself back together?

Twice so far. This isn't the first time.
I gave in to seduction; I fell into her trap.
I'm trying to let go, but the pain won't let it leave.
Sometimes it feels like I'm meant to go away;
"Sometimes it feels like a heart is no place to be singing from at all..."

Labyrinth

I've been here before.
I must be back tracking.
The twisting and turning corridors wrap around mercilessly.
Around every corner, a dead end, a pitfall, a new trap.
The confusing pathways aren't meant to be escaped.
I'm just a rate in a maze.

Which way do I go?
I'm exhausted. I'm famished. I'm parched.
I've been stumbling in circles for more than a week...maybe two?
It's been so long since I've seen the warming light of day!
I've nearly gone blind from peering down each dim hallway.
I try to listen for any trace of the outside world;
But all I ever hear is my own heavy breathing.
My hands are scarred and gnarled from clawing for freedom.

I'm getting desperate.

Every pointless step I take leads me closer to death.
On the outside, I was a big shot...
I had a family, a job, a home - a life!
But down here, my existence means nothing.
Death has no concern for who I am;
The Reaper simply awaits my final breath.
I can feel him creeping closer, his cold hand outstretched.
I madly stagger along, continuing my fruitless search for freedom.
I must find a way out...I have to escape!

Wait!
A soft glow at the end of the tunnel!
I run for the opening - fresh air, sunlight, freedom all await me!
I feel a pleasant breeze; I heart the restless ocean.
My eyes adjust as I get closer to the light.
Joyfully, I bound round the next corner to face the daylight!

...nothing.

I gaze down a dark, empty corridor leading into oblivion.
An illusion...
A mirage...

I fall to the ground and decide to wait for Death's inviting hand to carry me on.

Seasonal Sorrow

In winter, it's cold with lots of snow.
In spring, the trees and flowers grow.
In summer, it rains and cool winds blow.
In Autumn, I feel pain and sorrow.

I'm the only one who truly knows
Exactly how this story goes.

Now I'll tell you the reason why
My heart was broken, left to die.

September of 2007,
I met an angel who fell from heaven.

Magnificent beauty that was unmatched,
To her, my soul, it felt attached.

She liked me, and we had lots of fun;
I loved her more than anyone.

I pinched myself and tried to scream
To make sure it was not a dream.

I had the best time of my life;
I felt no pain, no hurt, no strife.

The month before, I felt depressed,
But here with her, I felt so blessed.

And all my sorrow was destroyed -
I honestly was overjoyed!

I thanked God for sending her to me;
Unfortunately, I did not see
That what would happen next would be
A terrible catastrophe.

October of that very year,
The point of no return drew near.

While we were talking one fine day,
She said she had something to say.

Unknowingly, the point grew near,
So I listened with an eager ear.

Then, at much to my surprise,
She told me it was all just lies.

She never liked me, I was just being used;
I felt so hopeless and confused.

She crushed my weak and fragile heart.
It was all a lie right from the start.

The month before, I felt depressed,
But here with her, I felt so blessed.

And all my sorrow was destroyed -
I honestly was overjoyed!

I thanked God for sending her to me;
Unfortunately, I did not see
That what would happen next would be
A terrible catastrophe.

October of that very year,
The point of no return drew near.

While we were talking one fine day,
She said she had something to say.

Unknowingly, the point grew near,
So I listened with an eager ear.

Then, at much to my surprise,
She told me it was all just lies.

She never liked me, I was just being used;
I felt so hopeless and confused.

She crushed my weak and fragile heart.
It was all a lie right from the start.

And last of all, I'll say if I must,
It took away my sense of trust.

Ever since that fateful day,
It's hard to believe what people say.

It's hard to even trust my friends...
The paranoia never ends!

As much as I tried to ignore,
The pain kept growing more and more.

My whole life ceased to be fair;
The burden was too much to bear.

Since then I've never been the same>
But who is there but me to blame?

It was my own fault, I couldn't see
That she lied about everything to me.

Now, listen to what I say to you
This poetic story is very true.

This poem tells the reason why
My life was changed by one small lie.

www.ingramcontent.com/pod-product-compliance
Lightning Source LLC
Chambersburg PA
CBHW051739130826
49812CB00033B/930
9789357210812